Mwâkwa
Talks to the Loon

Written and Illustrated by

DALE AUGER

HERITAGE

Heritage House Publishing Company Ltd.
heritagehouse.ca

Cataloguing information available from Library and Archives Canada
978-1-77203-487-5 (hardcover)
978-1-77203-488-2 (paperback)
978-1-77203-489-9 (ebook)

Edited by Don Gorman
Cree translation, glossary, and pronunciation guide by Billy-Joe Laboucan
Cover and interior book design by R-House Design and Setareh Ashrafologhalai

The interior of this book was produced on FSC®-certified, acid-free paper,
processed chlorine free, and printed with vegetable-based inks.

Heritage House gratefully acknowledges that the land on which we
live and work is within the traditional territories of the Lkwungen
(Esquimalt and Songhees), Malahat, Pacheedaht, Scia'new, T'Sou-ke,
and W̱SÁNEĆ (Pauquachin, Tsartlip, Tsawout, Tseycum) Peoples.

We acknowledge the financial support of the Government of Canada
through the Canada Book Fund (CBF) and the Canada Council for
the Arts, and the Province of British Columbia through the British
Columbia Arts Council and the Book Publishing Tax Credit.

28 27 26 25 24   1 2 3 4 5

Printed in China

This happened in a place
called Kitaskînaw, Our Land.

A young man named Kayâs—whose name means "Long Time Ago"—lived there. This young man had been given a Gift that made him a talented hunter: he knew the ways of the Beings he hunted.

Kayâs knew where to find onêwokâtîwak, the four-legged kind; pêyisêsak, the winged ones; and those that swim beneath the water, kinosîwak. He even knew how to talk with them in their languages—kaskihtâw tapîkiskwît opîkiskwîwiniyiwa.

Using his Gift, Kayâs provided food, shelter, and clothing for the People. Whenever the People were hungry, Kayâs would go hunting and bring them food.

The People felt grateful when Kayâs brought the food back to them and, over time, many others throughout the land came to know of his great hunting skills.

All the People spoke well of Kayâs because he was so skillful and so generous, ê-nihtâ mâcît ekwa ê-nihtâwasahkît, and the women always praised him as he walked through the village.

Kayâs loved the attention.

But pretty soon, Kayâs
loved the attention more
than he loved hunting.

After a while, Kayâs stopped getting up early to go hunting, choosing instead to stay in the village, walking back and forth, listening for the People's praise; ê-kî mistahitîyimisot ekwa ê-kihtimikanît.

Then the People started getting hungry, and they wondered why Kayâs wasn't hunting anymore.

The People stopped praising the young man and started to say to him, "You should go hunting instead of sitting around the village. The birchbark baskets and drying racks are empty. Namakîkway astîw waskwayoyâkanihk ekwa akwâwânihk. What will we eat? We are hungry. Ninohtîhkatânân."

Kayâs replied, "I can go hunting anytime
I want. I can find the Beings of Our Land
anytime I want, for I am a great hunter!"

So the next morning, Kayâs
awoke early and set off on a hunt.

Sadly, Kayâs came back that evening with no food.

Kayâs had lost his way, ê-kî-wanisihk, and he didn't know where to find the Beings anymore.

Kayâs could no longer speak with the four-legged kind, onêwokâtîwak; he didn't know where to look for the winged ones, pêyisêsak; and he couldn't find the Water Beings, onipîwâcihôwak, either.

Pretty soon Kayâs did not go out hunting at all. He just stayed inside his lodge, his omîkowâhpihk.

Kayâs did not want to come out and face the People, because he knew that he had lost his way, ê-kî-wanisihk, along with his Gift and his ability to provide food for the People.

Then one morning, Kayâs woke up and knew what he must do.

Kayâs walked straight over to the Elders' lodge, went in, and sat to the side in silence.

Kihtîyayak, the Elders, did not greet Kayâs when he came in, as they had been watching him from a distance for some time, and they knew what he had come for.

They continued to say nothing and just let him sit there, quietly thinking about his situation.

After some time, one of the Elders leaned over to him and said, "Nôsisim. Tân'si. Grandson, hello." Then the Elders asked Kayâs to sit with them: "Âstam pîwîtapiminân ôta."

"Grandson," they said, "we are glad that you've come. We have been watching you and we know that you've lost your way and your ability to hunt."

The Elders then prayed with Kayâs, offering him the power of the Loon Spirit.

Before long, they stood, and one of them told Kayâs, "Go down to the lake and call nikwîmîy, your same-spirit.

Go down by the water and call on Mwâkwa, the Loon, to help you. The Loon owes us, because once we caught him in our net by accident. But we set him free because we pitied him. So go ask him to help you, kakwîcim ta wîcihisk."

"Mwââââkwaaaa . . ."

So Kayâs went down
to the lake, stood by the
side of the water and
called out to Mwâkwa,
the Loon:

Mwââââââââkwaaaaaaaaa . . ."
. . . âââkwaaaa . . .

And just like that, Mwâkwa appeared. In a very
strong and grouchy voice the Loon said, **"What is it?
Why do you bother me?"**

This response made Kayâs a little nervous, but
still he answered Mwâkwa, saying, "The Elders sent
me here to ask you for help. They say you owe them
a favour in order to repay your debt to them and
honour their ways."

"Yes, yes, yes," said Mwâkwa. "Aniki kihtîyayak,
those Old Ones. I had forgotten that I owed them for
the Gift they gave to me so long ago—the Gift of my
freedom. **Now, what is it? Tell me what you want."**

"My People are hungry and I can no longer provide for them anymore, as I have lost my way and have forgotten how to use the talents—the Gift—that I was given," said Kayâs. "If I do not find my way again, they will not have any food to eat."

Listening to the young man, Mwâkwa decided that he would help Kayâs rediscover his ability to hunt and feed the People.

The Loon then dove under
the water and into the green light
below to ask onipîwâcihôwak,
those Beings that swim beneath
the water, if they would help the
young man.

After some time, Mwâkwa
returned. He told Kayâs that
onipîwâcihôwak, the Water
Beings, had agreed to help
him feed the People.

Mwâkwa then said to Kayâs, "They say that you should go where the water is shallow and the trees are plenty. There kinosîwak, the Fish, will come to shore. They will give themselves to you and the People.

"But in return, they ask for two things. The first is that you hold a large feast to honour onipîwâcihôwak, the Water Beings, and all of the Beings that you and your people depend upon for food, shelter, and clothing. You must call on all the People to come to this feast, to dance and rejoice in the harvest that they have been provided with. You must do so every year, from this time on.

"The second thing is that you sing a song at the feast that will honour the spirits of kinosîwak, the Fish, and all of the Beings that you hunt, who have given of themselves in order to feed you and the People."

And just like that, Mwâkwa was gone.

After Mwâkwa had spoken, Kayâs was very happy. He ran to tell the Elders what Mwâkwa had said.

Upon hearing this, kihtîyayak, the Old Ones, called on all the People to go down to the shore of the lake, where the water was shallow and the trees were plenty.

When they arrived, the Fish were there, giving themselves to the People just as they had told Mwâkwa they would do when the Loon talked with them under the water, in the green light.
The People happily—and thankfully—gathered the Fish.

That night there was a
great feast.
The People danced to
honour onipîwâcihôwak,
the Water Beings, and all of
the Beings that the People
depended upon for food,
shelter, and clothing, as
Mwâkwa had told them to do.

Kayâs lifted his drum and sang to honour the Fish spirits, kinosîwak, and all of the Beings that he was to hunt throughout his life.

The Elders were happy now that Kayâs was again a gifted and talented hunter who had finally shown them respect and honoured their ways.

The Beings that Kayas hunted—onêwokâtîwak, the four-legged kind; pêyisêsak, the winged ones; and even those that swim beneath the water, kinosîwak—were also happy because the People kept their promise to honour them with dancing and singing, year after year.

Kayâs was happy because he knew he had found his way again. On the water, Mwâkwa was dancing, singing, and happy too.

Both Kayâs and Mwâkwa felt free,
for they had repaid their debts and
come to realize that one's Gifts may
be lost if they are not honoured and
cherished.

CREE WORDS AND PHRASES	PRONUNCIATION	ENGLISH TRANSLATION
akwâwân	*ugwaawaan*	drying rack
astam pîwîtapiminân ôta	*aastum peeweetapiminaan*	come and sit here with us
ê-kî mistahitîyimisot ekwa ê-kihtimikanît	*ee-gee mistahiteeyimisot egwa eegeekihtimiganeet*	he was proud and lazy
ê-kî-wanisihk	*eegeewanisihk*	he had lost his way
ê-nihtâ mâcît ekwa ê-nihtâwasahkît	*eenihtaa macheet egwa eenihtaawusuhkeet*	a skillful and generous hunter
kakwîcim ta wîcihisk	*kukweechim ta weechihisk*	ask for his help
kaskihtâw tapîkiskwît opîkiskwîwiniyiwa	*kuskihtaaw tapeekiskweet opeekiskweewinee-yiwa*	he was able speak in their languages
kayâs	*kayaas*	long time ago
kihtîyayak	*kihteeyayak*	Elders
kinosîwak	*kinoseewak*	those that swim beneath the water; fish
kitaskînaw	*kituskeenaw*	Our Land
mîkowâhp	*meegowaahp*	lodge
mwâkwa	*mwaagwa*	loon
namakîkway astîw waskwayoyâkanihk ekwa akwâwânihk	*na mugeekway usteew wuskwayoyaagunihk egwa ugwaanihk*	birchbark baskets and drying racks are empty
nikwîmiy	*nigweemee*	your same-spirit
ninohtîhkatânân	*ninohteehkataa-naan*	we are hungry
nôsisim	*noosisim*	grandson
omîkowâhpihk	*omeegowaahpihk*	his lodge
onêwokâtîwak	*oneewokaateewak*	four-legged kind
onipîwâcihôwak	*onipeewaachihoo-wak*	Water Beings; Beings that swim beneath the water
oyâkan	*oyaagun*	plate, basket
pêyisêsak	*paayiseesak*	winged ones; birds
pôskîyâkan	*pooskeyaagun*	bowl
tân'si	*taansi*	hello
waskway	*wusk wu y*	birchbark

DALE AUGER (1958–2008) was a Sakaw Cree artist and storyteller from the Bigstone Cree Nation in northern Alberta. He was born in High Prairie, Alberta, near that province's second-largest body of water, Lesser Slave Lake. He attended the Alberta College of Art and the University of Calgary, obtaining a master's degree in education and a PhD in education. *Mwâkwa Talks to the Loon* was named Aboriginal Children's Book of the Year at the 2006 Anskohk Aboriginal Literature Festival and Book Awards and also received the 2007 R. Ross Annett Award for Children's Literature.